Tips

▸ Keep your child's supplies in a container so that everything is close at hand.

▸ Explain directions before your child begins a new type of activity.

▸ Show your child how the illustrations help show what to do.

▸ Encourage your child to pick up and throw away all scraps when a project is finished.

Supplies

▸ scissors

▸ glue stick or paste

▸ crayons or colored pencils

▸ marking pens

▸ pencil

▸ clear tape

▸ some projects may require additional supplies

Table of Contents

The Never-Bored Kid Book • EMC 6300 • © Evan-Moor Corp.

Teddy Bear

Trace and color the other side of the Teddy Bear.

Bear Puzzle

Cut and glue.

glue

glue

glue

Bear Tracker

Help Mother and Baby Bear find the flowers.

10 Little Bear Cubs

Cut and glue together.

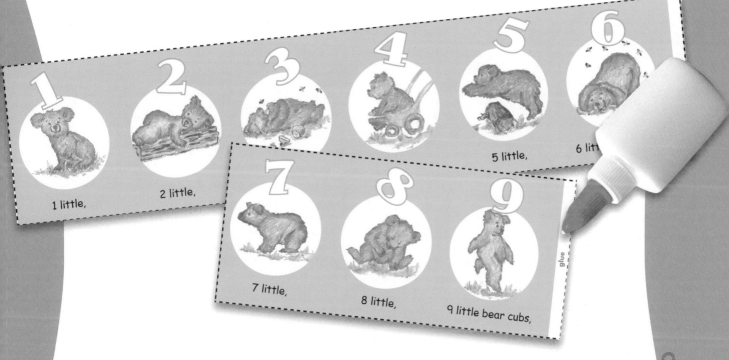

1 little,

2 little,

3

4

5 little,

6 litt

7 little,

8 little,

9 little bear cubs,

glue

1 little,

2 little,

3 little bear cubs,

glue

8

4 little,

5 little,

6 little bear cubs,

glue

7 little,

8 little,

9 little bear cubs,

glue

10 Cubs in a row

Cut and glue.
Put it on.

glue

glue

My Bear Headband

glue

glue

The Never-Bored Kid Book • EMC 6300 • © Evan-Moor Corp.

Dress the Sunny Day Bear

Cut out the clothes.
Dress the bear.

It's sunny! It's sunny.
Let's go out to play.
Put on sandals.
Grab your hat.
We'll have fun today.

14

Dress the Snowy Day Bear

It's snowing! It's snowing.
Let's go out to play.
Put on mittens.
Grab your scarf.
We'll have fun today.

16

Match the snowflakes.

Bear Houses

Trace the lines to the bear houses.
Help the bears get home.

A Bear Hug

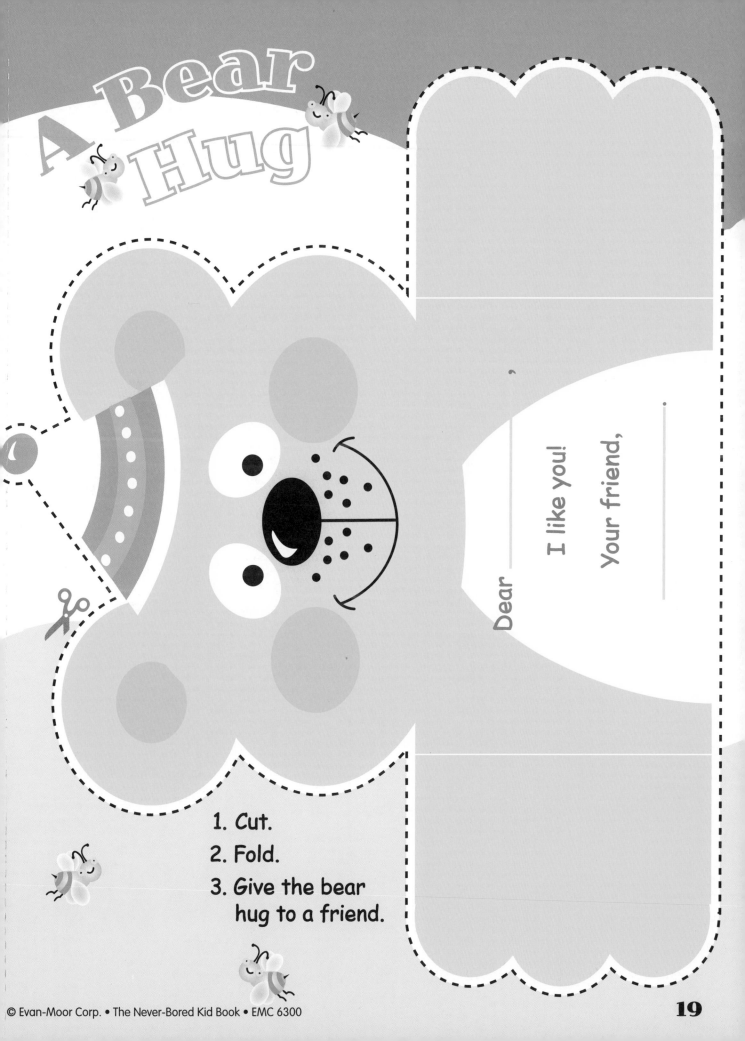

Dear _____

I like you!

Your friend,

_____

1. Cut.
2. Fold.
3. Give the bear hug to a friend.

20

Rabbits

Color the pictures.

1 2 3 4 5 !

I caught a hare alive.

6 7 8 9 10 !

I let it go again.

Hare in the Rain

Connect the dots.
Color the hare.

The Never-Bored Kid Book • EMC 6300 • © Evan-Moor Corp.

Many Rabbits

fold

1

fold

2

fold

3

Cut out the rabbits.
Set them on a table.

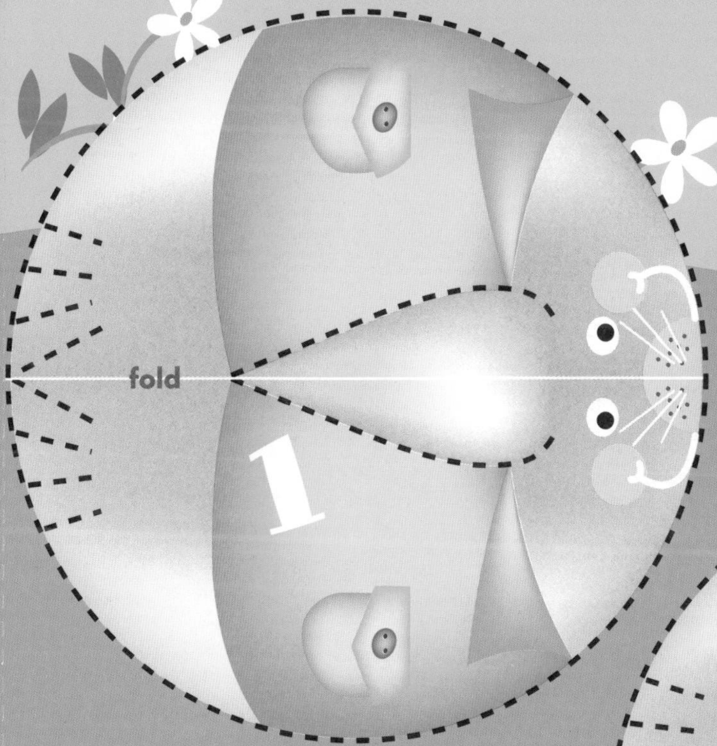

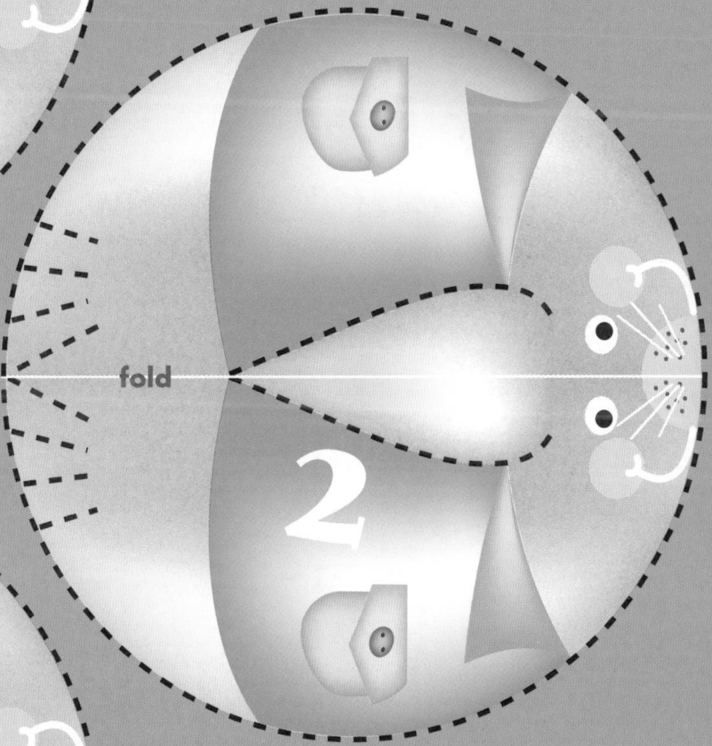

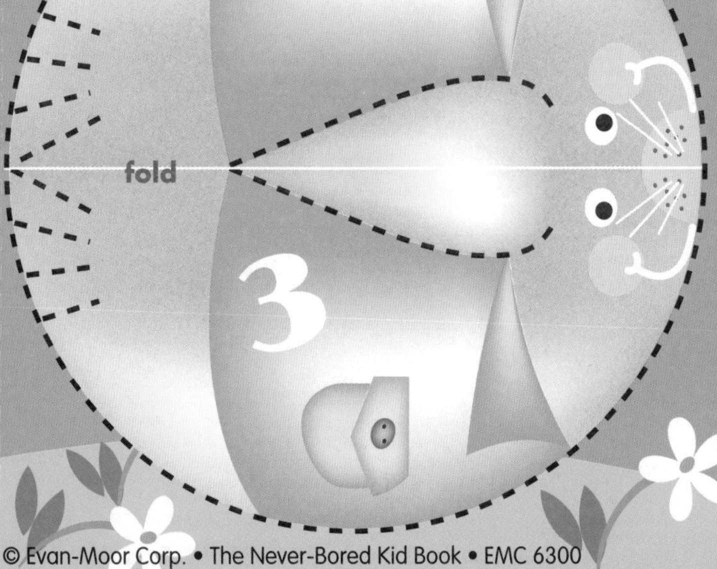

Bunny Puzzle

Cut.
Glue on the next page.

26

Bunny Puzzle

glue

glue

glue

glue

Front and Back

Match.

Bunny Puppets

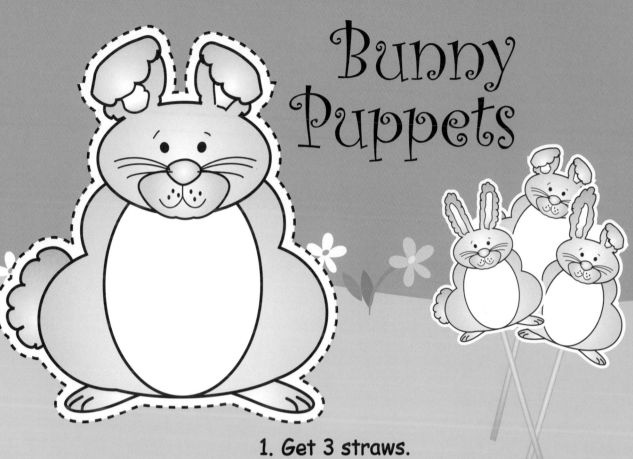

1. Get 3 straws.
2. Cut out the bunnies.
3. Glue them to the straws.

My Wagon

glue

fold

glue

Cut out the parts.
Fold up and glue the wagon.
Add the wheels and handle.
Put the pets inside.

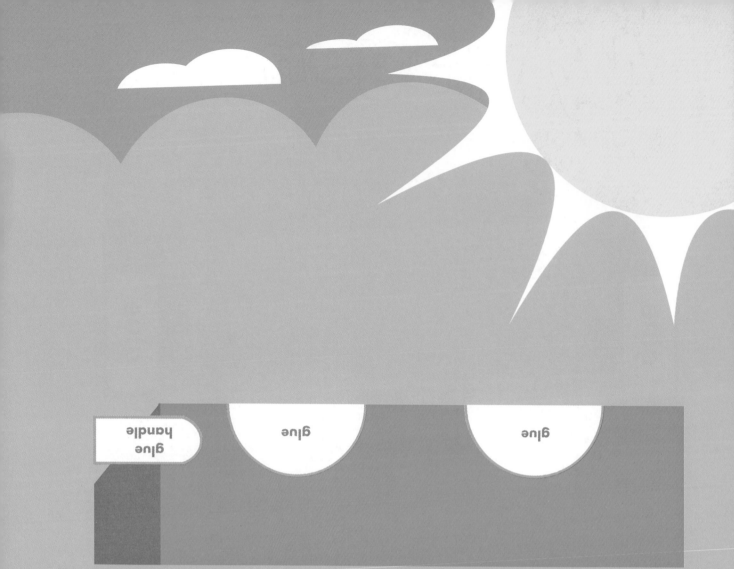

What Fits in My Wagon?

Circle what fits in your wagon.

Which Is Different?

Find the one that is different.

To the Park

Draw a line to the park.

Wagon Dot-to-Dot

Connect the dots.
Color the picture.

red

orange

green

purple

yellow

gray

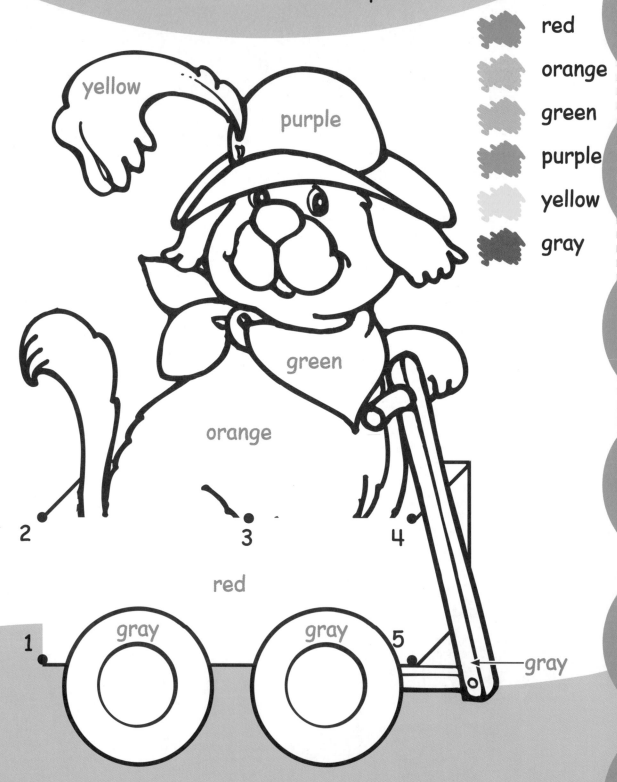

Rain, Rain

Complete the umbrella.
Color the picture.
Make raindrops.

It's raining! It's raining!
Put on your rain boots fast!
Go splash in the puddles.
Hurry while they last.

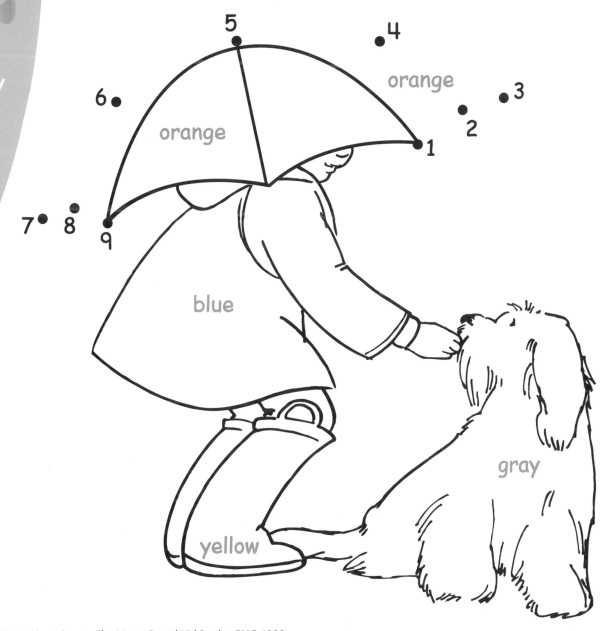

A Pair of Umbrellas

Find 2 the same.

Cut.
Fold.

Glue on page 41.

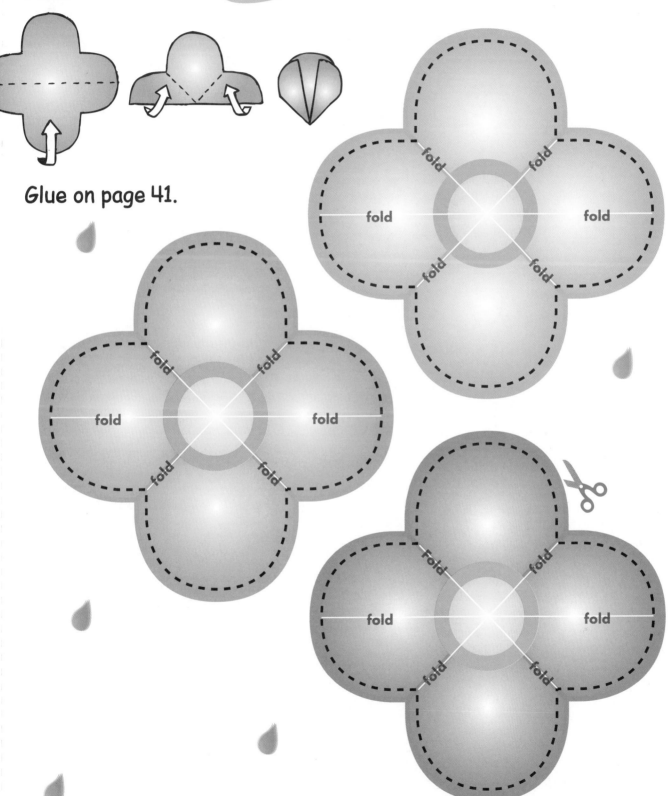

It's Raining

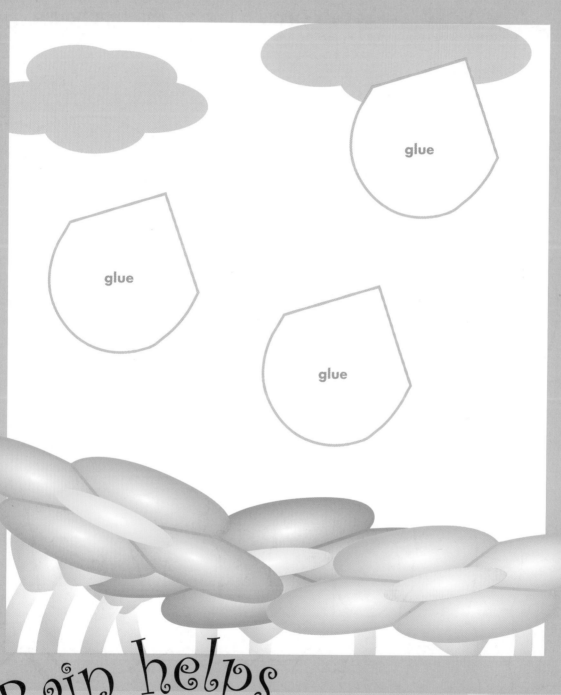

glue

glue

glue

Rain helps flowers grow.

Hurry Home

Draw a line to the birdhouse.

What Is Missing?

glue

glue

glue

Cut and glue.

Puddle Fun

Trace the line.

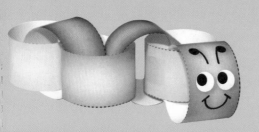

Creepy Caterpillar

Cut and glue the rings together.

glue

glue

glue

glue

glue

glue

Hungry Caterpillar

Draw a line to the flowers.

Start ➡

End ➡

Who Is It?

Color the ⊙s in green.

I see a _____.

Nibble, Nibble, Caterpillar

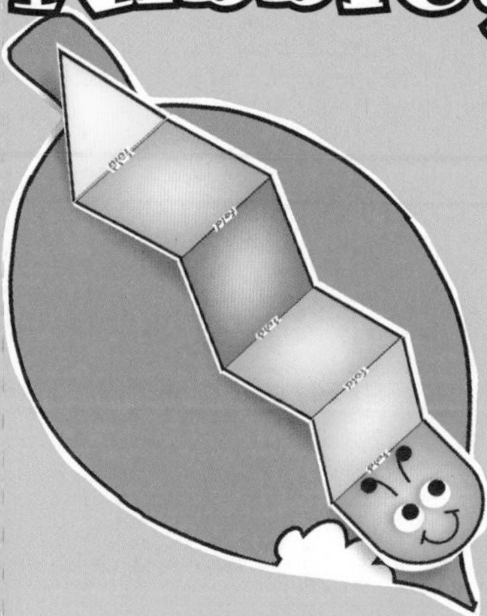

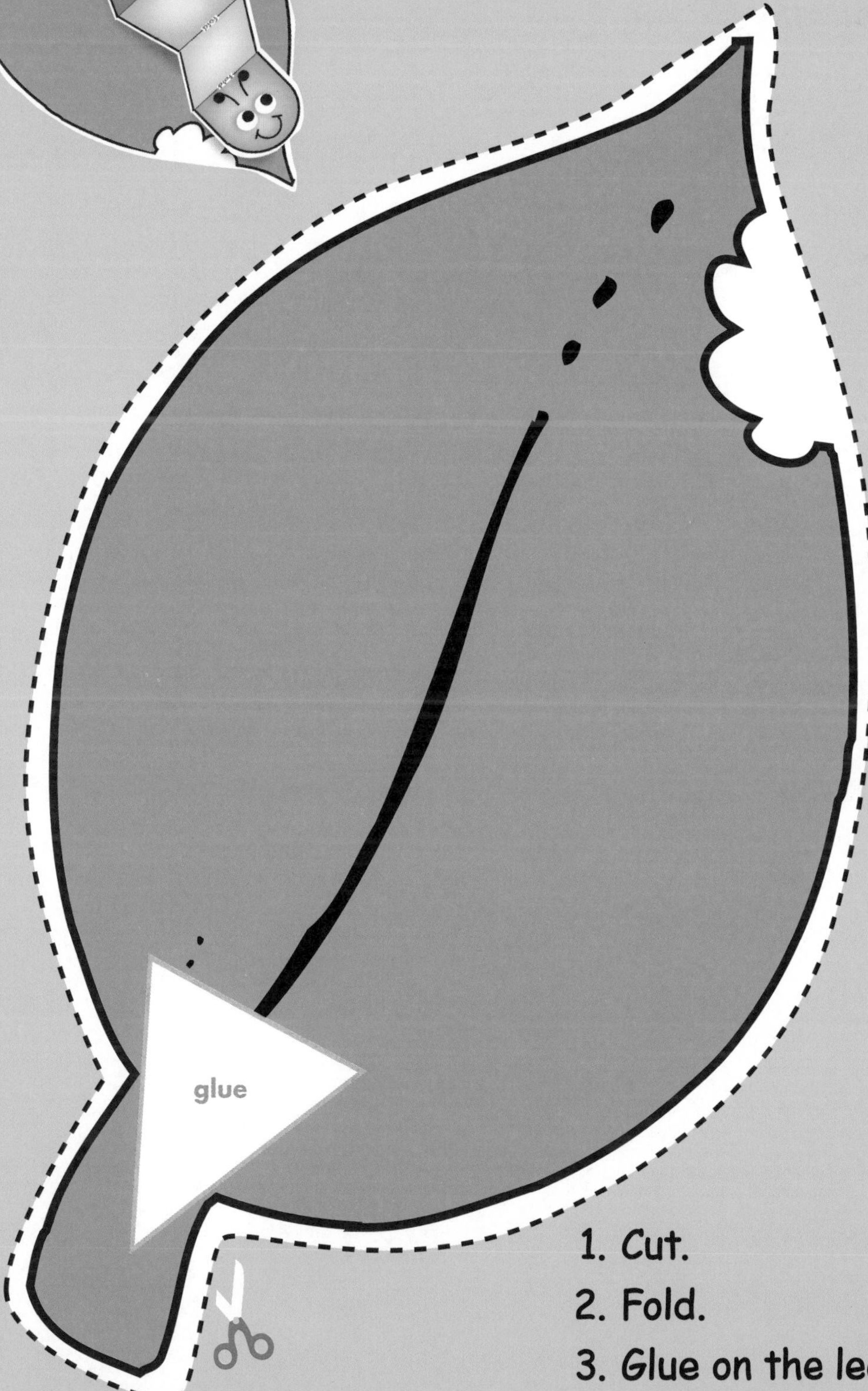

fold

fold

fold

fold

fold

1. Cut.
2. Fold.
3. Glue on the leaf.

glue

Caterpillar Puzzle

Cut and glue on the next page.

51

glue

glue

glue

glue

Find the Caterpillars

Color the caterpillars you find.

I see ⬤ caterpillars.

The Never-Bored Kid Book • EMC 6300 • © Evan-Moor Corp.

Is Anyone Home?

Cut and glue.

glue

glue

glue

glue

glue

To Grandma's House

Draw a line to the house.

start

end

Start at 1.
Make Pig's house.

Little Pig's House

58

Cut.
Glue to the next page.

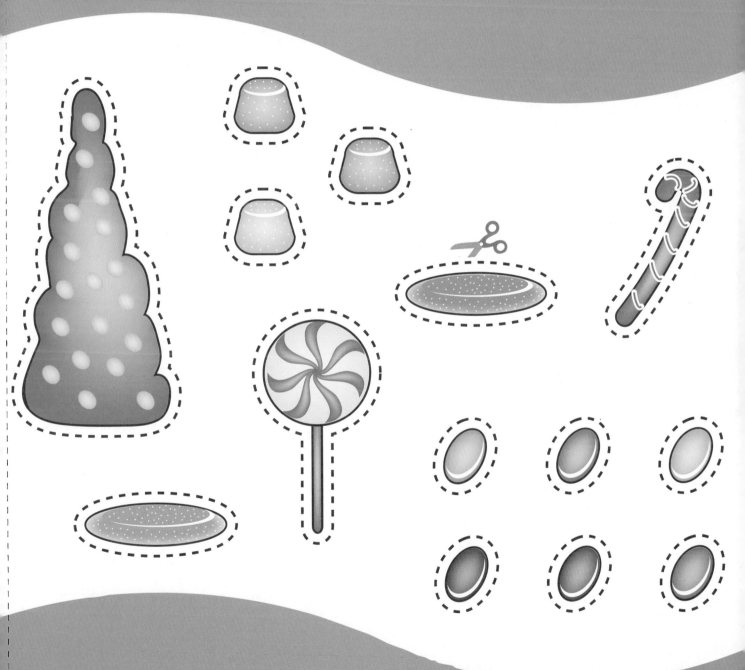

Snowman

Color the picture.

Make a Snowman

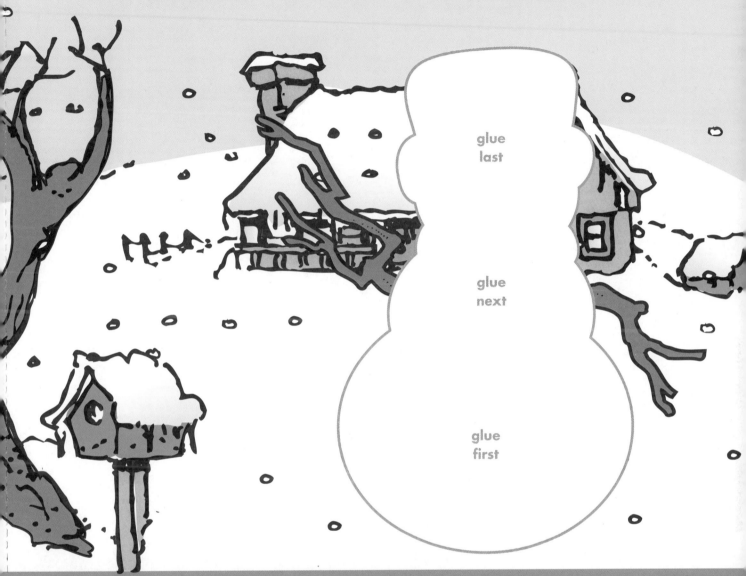

glue
last

glue
next

glue
first

Cut and glue.

Melting Snowman

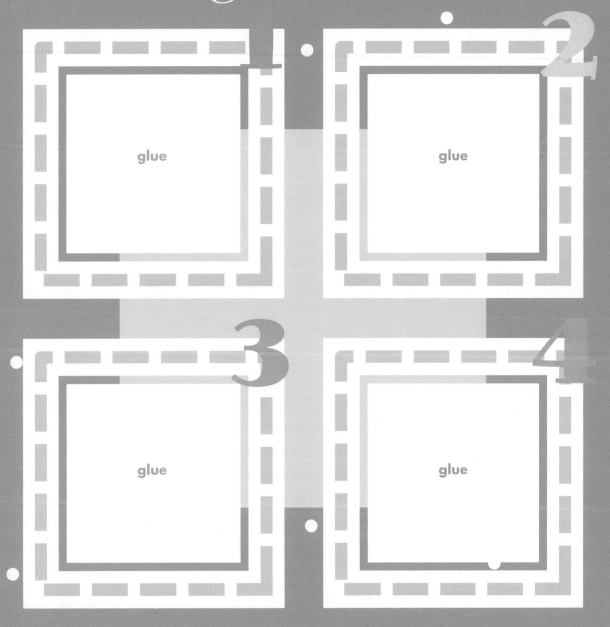

1. glue
2. glue
3. glue
4. glue

Cut. Glue in order.

Draw and color.
Copy the snowman.

Two in the Snow

Find the Twin

Circle the 2 snowmen that are the same.

 The Never-Bored Kid Book • EMC 6300 • © Evan-Moor Corp.

Elephant

Trace and color.

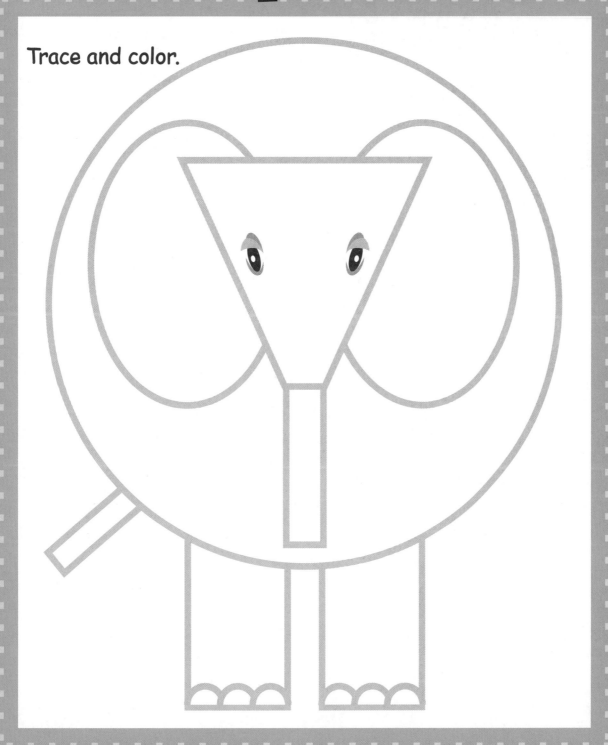

yellow   red   orange   blue   green

Paper Tube

Get a toilet paper tube.
Cut out the parts.
Glue them to the tube
following the steps.

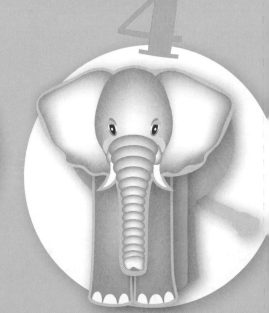

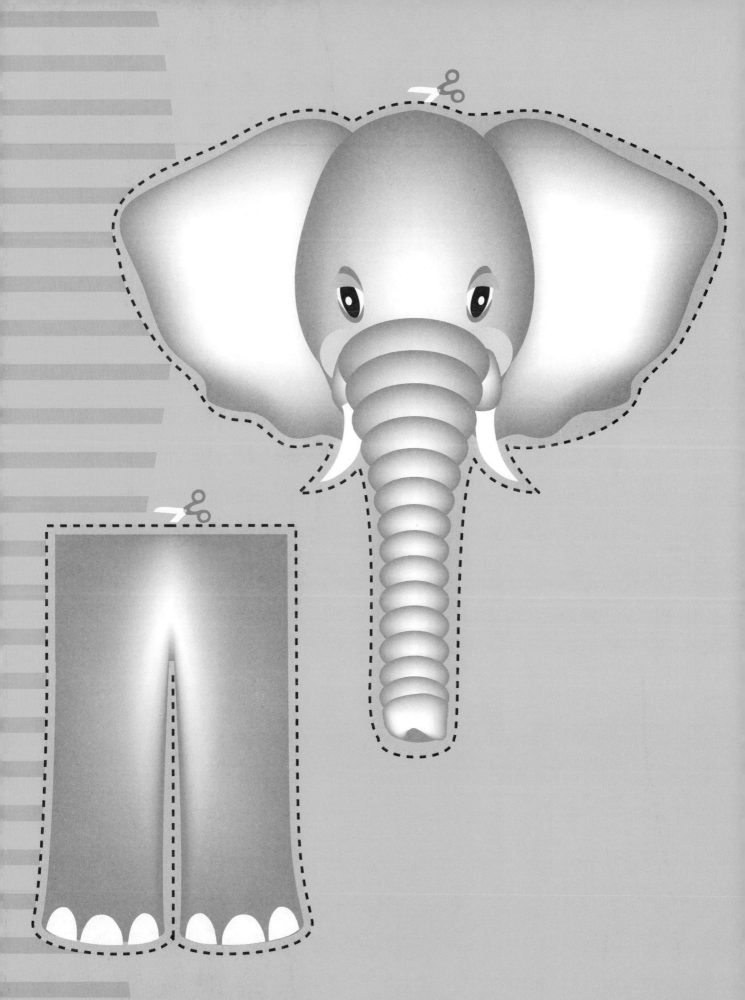

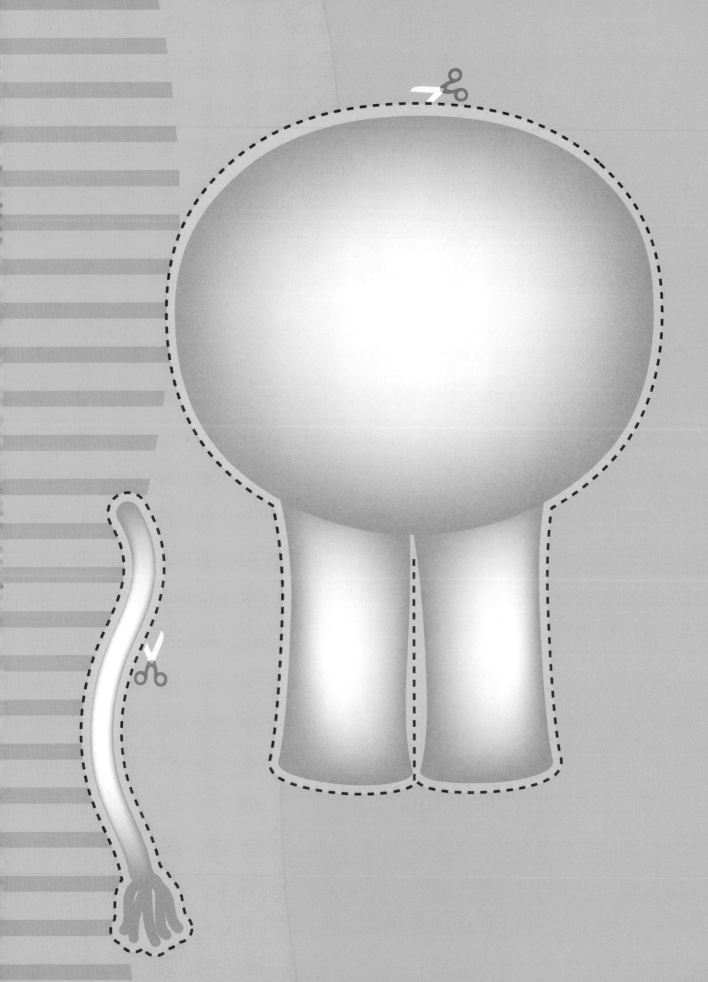

74

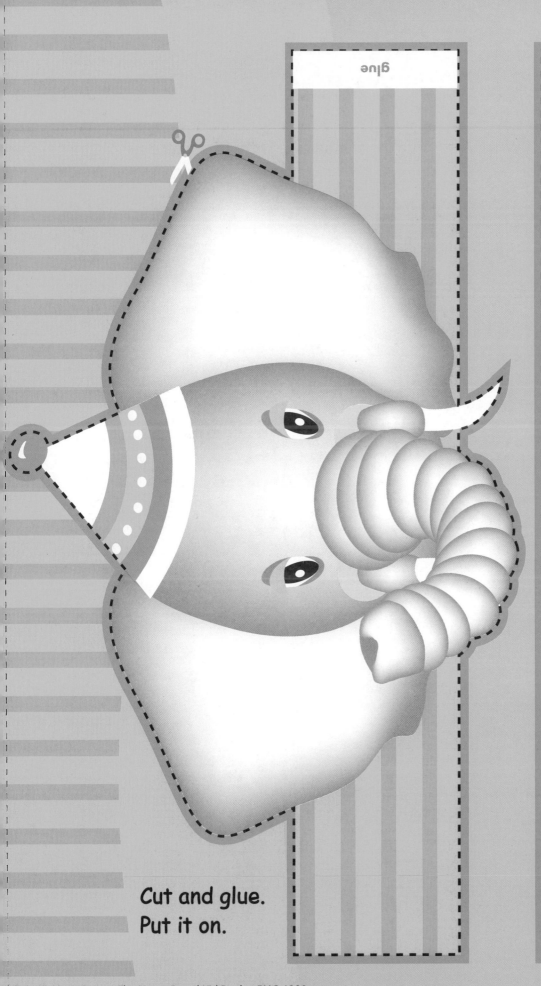

glue

glue

My Elephant Headband

Cut and glue.
Put it on.

76

Circus Elephant Puzzle

Cut and glue on the next page.

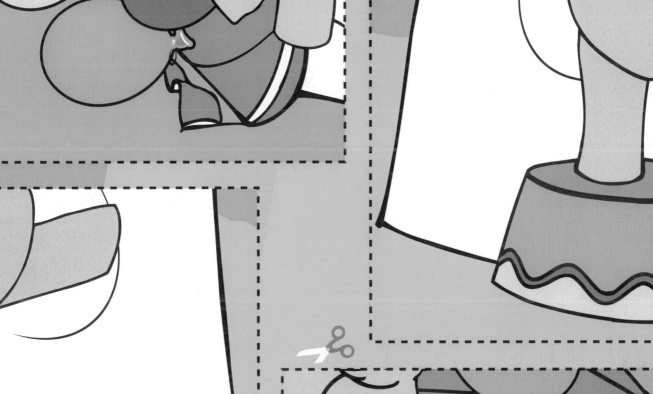

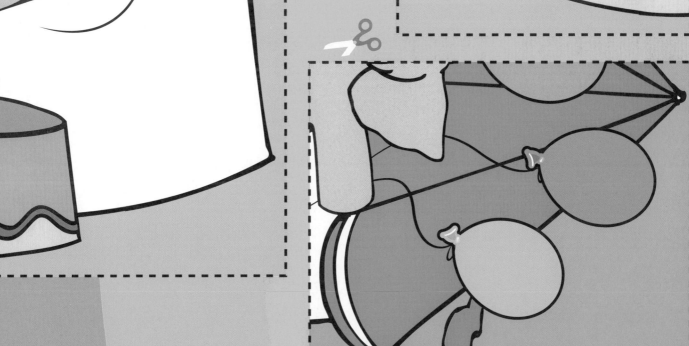

78

Circus Elephant

glue

glue

glue

glue

Who Is the Driver?

Match.

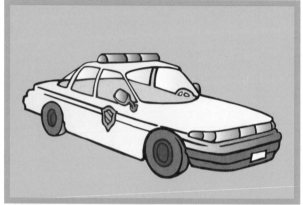

My Car

Cut and glue.

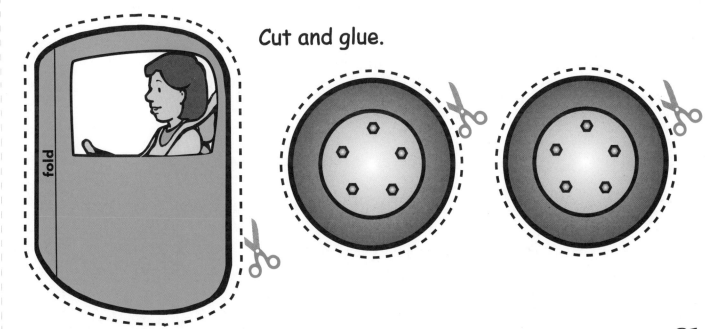

Pop-Up Card

Cut and fold.

Glue.

fold 2

fold 1   fold 1

cut   cut

glue
truck

fold 2

See the truck.
Go truck, go.

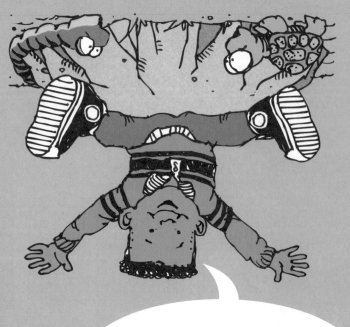

Wow! A Pop-Up Truck!

See the truck go.

Wheels Go Round

How many 🟦 can you find? ☐

How many 🔺 can you find? ☐

How many ⚪ can you find? ☐

How many ⬜ can you find? ☐

85

Time for School

Start at the
school bus.

Stop

Stop

Stop

Stop

Stop

School

← End

86

The Never-Bored Kid Book • EMC 6300 • © Evan-Moor Corp.

Fly Away

Cut and glue.

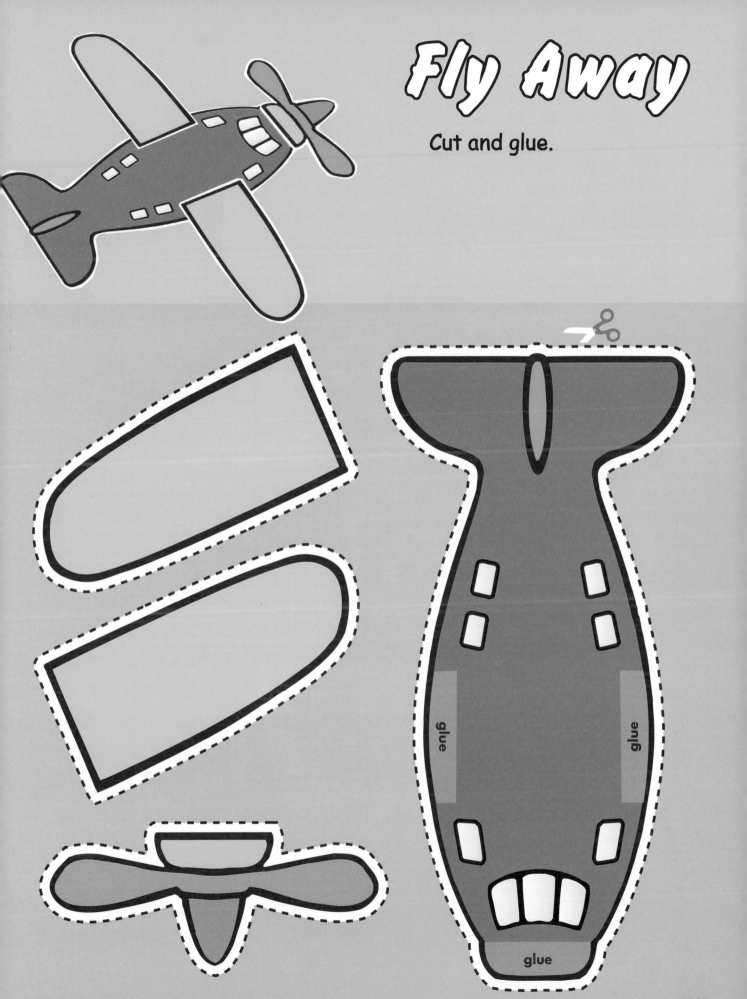

glue

glue

glue

Trace and color the pets.

What pet do you like best? _____

Doghouses

Trace the lines to the doghouses.
Help the dogs get home.

The Never-Bored Kid Book • EMC 6300 • © Evan-Moor Corp.

Make a Long Dog

Cut it out.
Glue the pieces together.

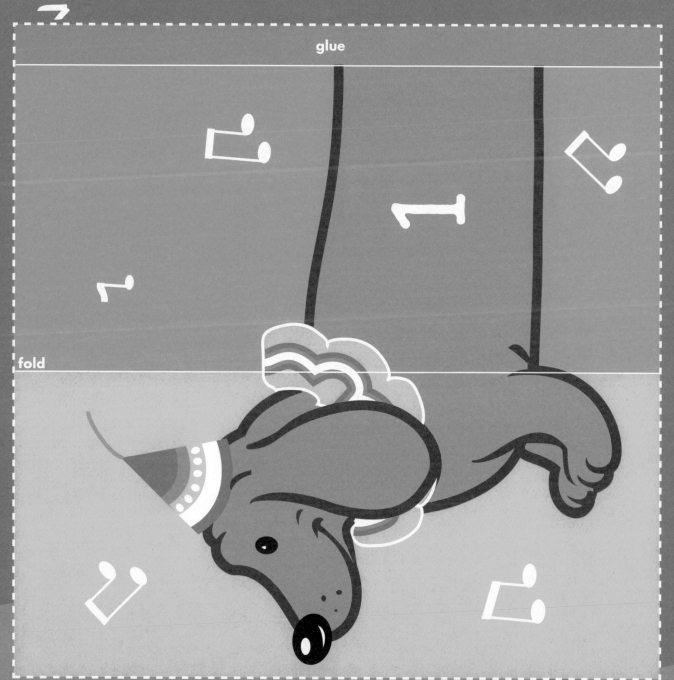

94

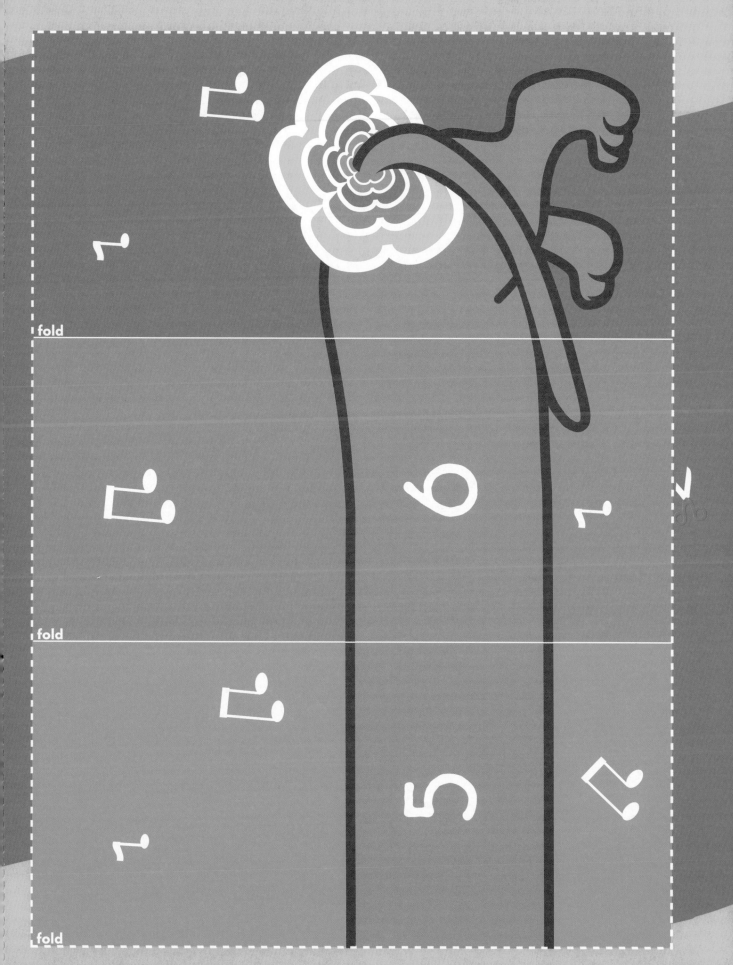

Kitty Cat

Circle what the kitty likes.

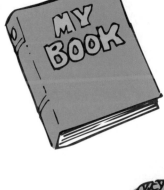

My Dog

Circle what the dog likes.

Pet Puppets

Get 5 straws.
Cut out the puppets.
Glue them to the straws.

Pet Homes

Cut and glue.

Hello Bird

Find 2 the same.

Match.

Lots of Pets

103

Draw a Cat

Trace and color the other side of the cat.

Kim's Lost Kitten

Help Kim find her kitten.

Doggy Bath

Connect the dots.
Color the tub.

Bird Puzzle

Cut and glue on the next page.

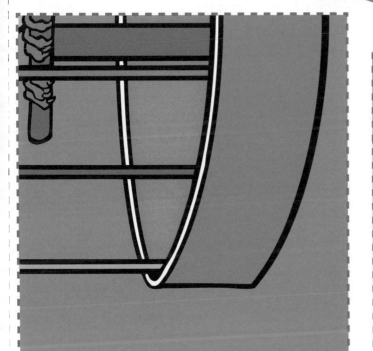

glue

glue

glue

glue

Pet Fish

Trace the fish.
Color them.

The Zoo

Cut out the scenes.
Glue them on pages 114 and 115.

Who Wears What?

Match.

glue

glue

glue

114

Giraffe

Help the giraffe find his dinner.

The Never-Bored Kid Book • EMC 6300 • © Evan-Moor Corp.

Elephant

Connect the dots.
Color the elephant.

Help Hippo

Trace and color.

Monkey

Take the monkey to the treat.

Rainbows

Color the rainbow.

red

orange

yellow

green

blue

purple

The Never-Bored Kid Book • EMC 6300 • © Evan-Moor Corp.

Make a Rainbow

Cut.
Glue them on the cloud on page 123.

glue	glue	glue	glue	glue	glue

122

124

My Rainbow

**Cut. Fold.
Read the story.**

My book: Jessica

1

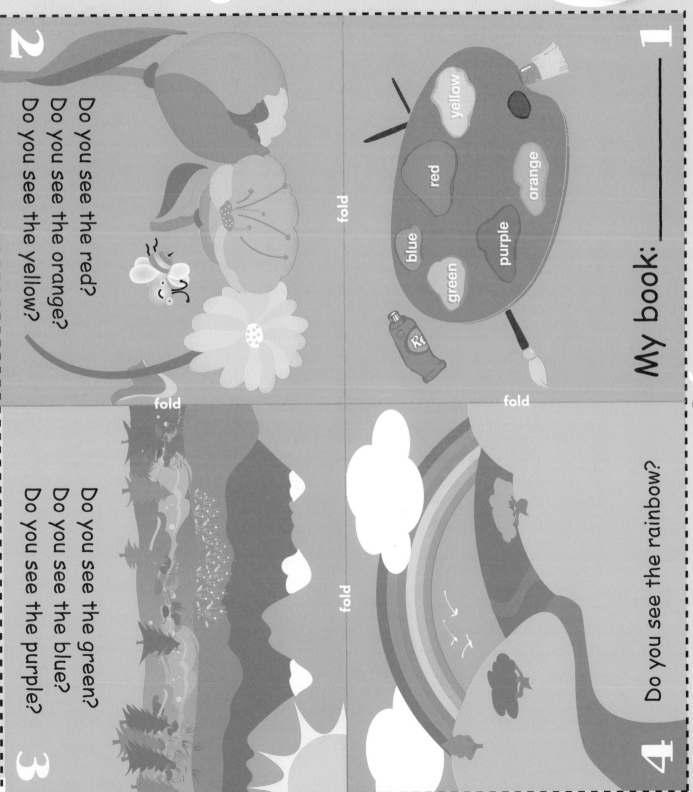

1

My book: _____

2

Do you see the red?
Do you see the orange?
Do you see the yellow?

3

Do you see the green?
Do you see the blue?
Do you see the purple?

4

Do you see the rainbow?

fold

fold

fold

fold

Cut and glue.

Mouse

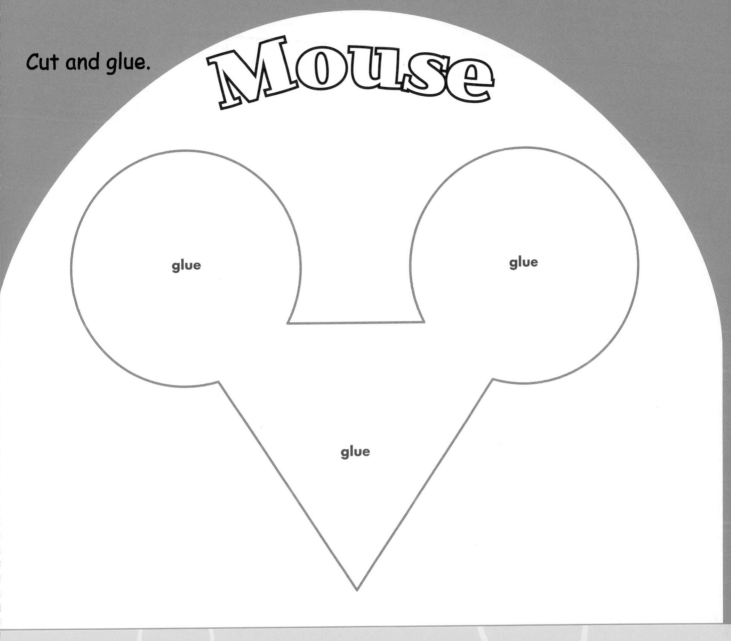

glue

glue

glue

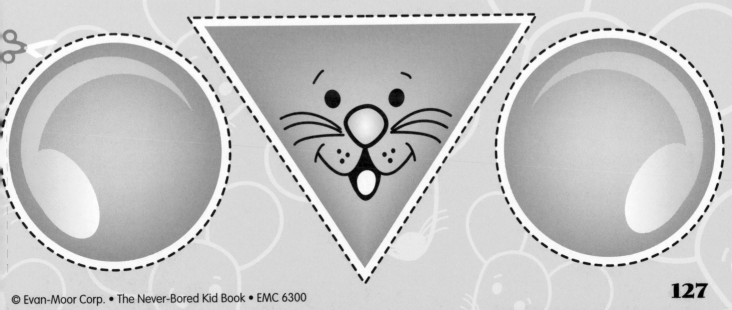

Color the Funny Mouse

The Never-Bored Kid Book • EMC 6300 • © Evan-Moor Corp.

My Little Mouse

1. Cut.
2. Fold.

3. Glue.

glue
tail

fold   fold   fold

glue   glue
ear   ear

129

More Mouse

Draw what is missing.

Hungry Mouse

Start at 1.
Connect the dots.
Color it all.

The Never-Bored Kid Book • EMC 6300 • © Evan-Moor Corp.

Mouse Puppet

Cut and glue.
Put it on your hand.

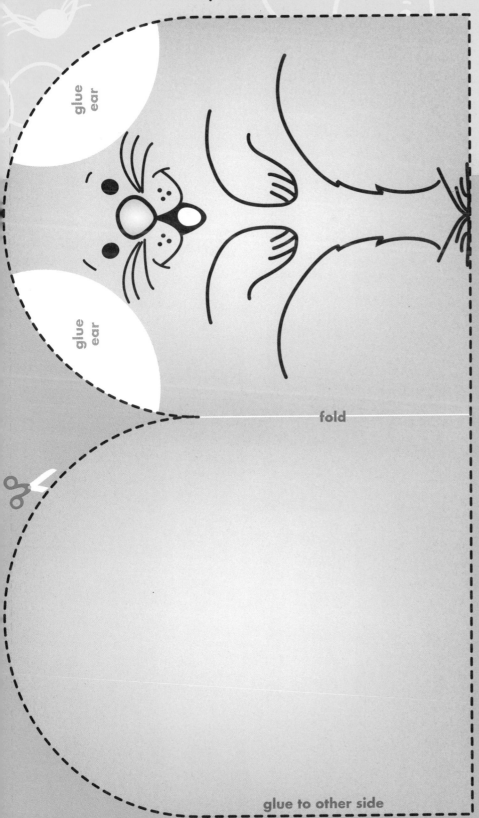

glue ear

glue ear

fold

glue to other side

134

Hickory, Dickory, Dock!

Cut out the clock.

up

down

Hickory, dickory, dock!
The mouse ran up the clock.
The clock struck one,
And down he run.
Hickory, dickory, dock!

Hickory, Dickory, Dock!

Cut out the mouse.
Fold on the lines.

1

Add a yarn tail.

2 Attach hands and pendulum to clock using fasteners.

fold **fold**

fold **fold**

Fold **fold**

tick! tock!

3 Put the mouse on the clock.
Go up.
Go down.
Hickory, dickory, dock.

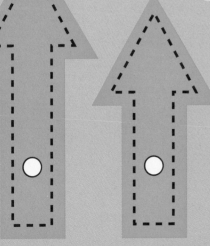

Color
the fruit.

■ red

■ purple

■ green

■ yellow

Yummy Fruit

green

green

red

red

yellow

purple

Good for You

Connect the dots.
Start at 1.
Stop at 10.

green

1• •10 •9

•8

2•

red

•7

3•

•6

4• •5

1 2 3 4 5 6 7 8 9 10

140

Circle the different one in each row.

Look
Alikes

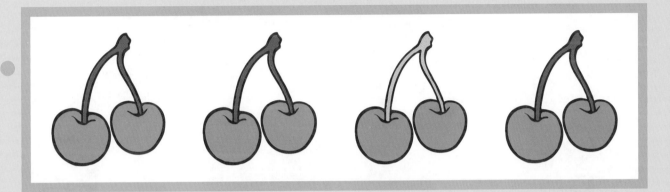

My Apple Tree

Cut and glue on the tree.

Cut and glue on page 142.

Spider Home

Cut out and glue on page 147.

Spider Home

glue	glue
glue	glue

A web is a home for a spider.

Color the rooster.

The Never-Bored Kid Book • EMC 6300 • © Evan-Moor Corp.

Cut and fold on
the lines.

Glue the chicks under
Mother's wings.

Find Red Hen's eggs.

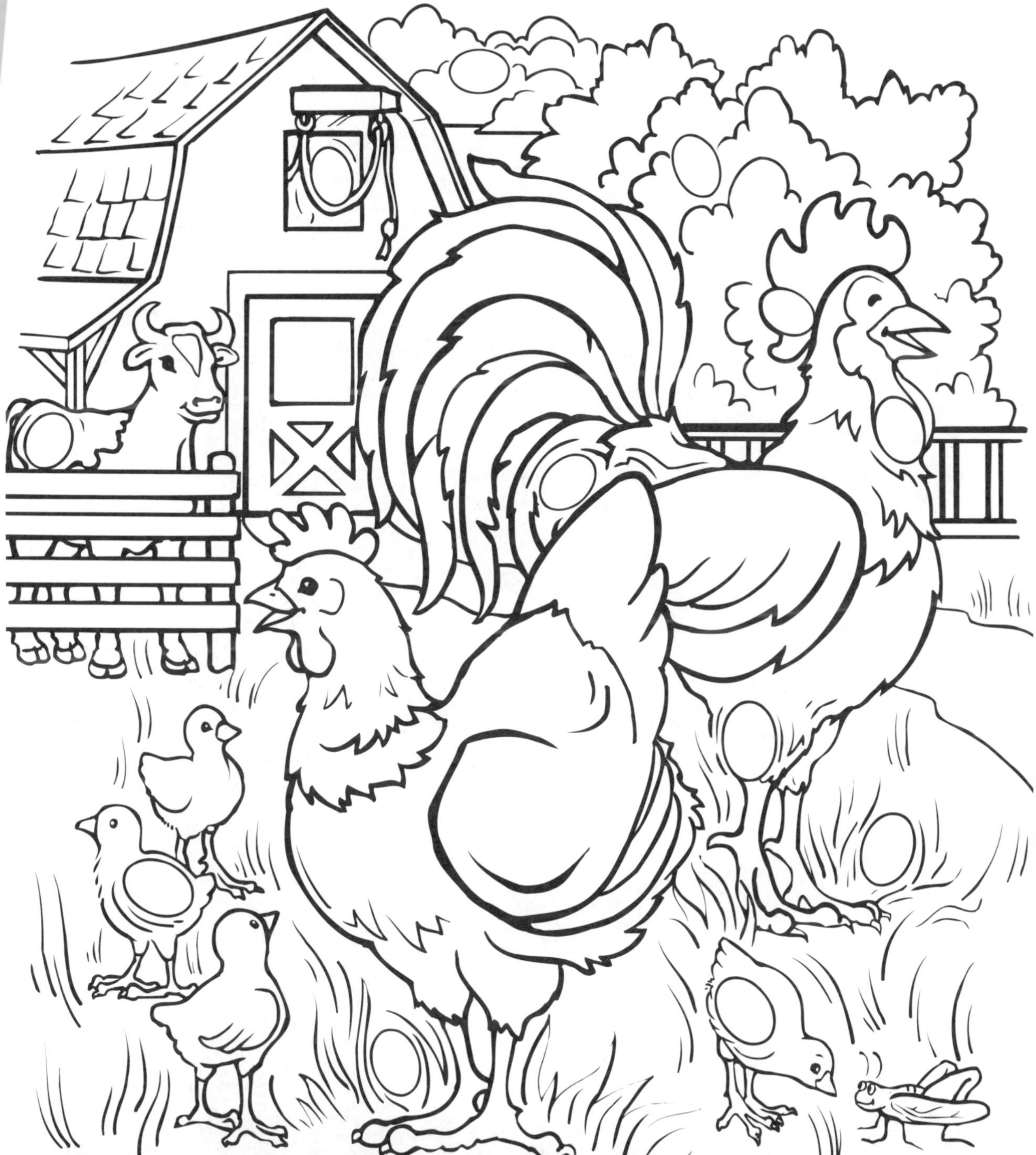

How many s did you find?

To Mother Hen's Nest

Draw a line to the nest.

start

end

Trace the other side.
Color it.

Answer Key

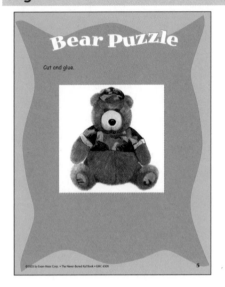

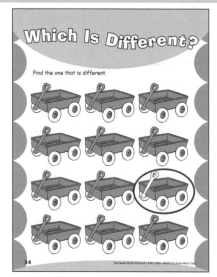

Page 44

Page 47

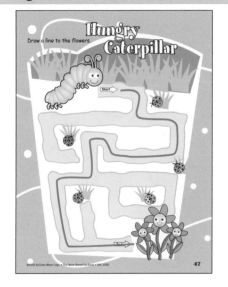

Page 48

Page 53

Page 54

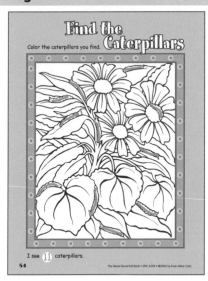

Page 55

Page 57

Page 58

Page 63

156

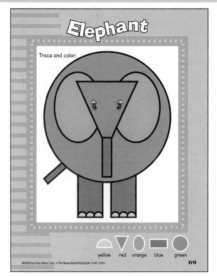

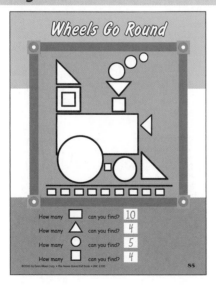

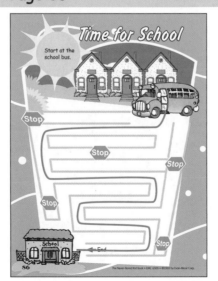

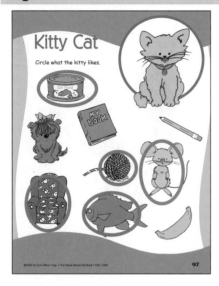

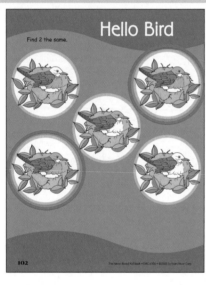

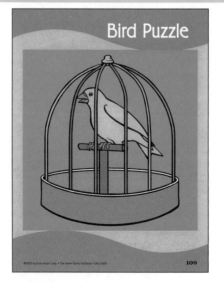